Curios
of
Staffordshire

A County Guide
to the Unusual

by

Ros Prince

S.B. Publications

For Andy and my parents

First published in 1992 by S.B. Publications
Unit 2, The Old Station Yard, Pipe Gate, Nr. Market Drayton
Shropshire TF9 4HY

British Library Cataloguing in Publication Data
available from the British Library on request

ISBN 1-85770-012-0

Typeset and printed by Delmar Press (Colour Printers) Ltd., Nantwich, Cheshire

CONTENTS

CONTENTS

Front Cover: The smallest telegraph pole, Woodseaves.
Half Title Page: 'The Fosser' at Rocester.
Back Cover: Bagot's Goats at Blithfield Hall.

ACKNOWLEDGEMENTS

First of all to Steve Benz, of S.B. Publications, whose idea it was. To Louis Livesey, former Director of Libraries, Arts and Archives, and his now-retired deputy Geoff Bradley, both of whom are responsible for pushing me into writing originally; and to all the staff at various libraries throughout the county who have helped in my research, especially Judy Warrillow and Chris Budworth. Finally, to Alan Clarke, who took all the best photographs, and Lucy Benz for the photograph on page 28.

Edited by Frank Rhodes.

INTRODUCTION

Staffordshire is such a varied county, stretching from the wild North Staffordshire Moors down almost to the heart of the industrialised West Midlands, that it simply has to be bursting with interesting little follies, eccentricities, curiosities and bits of industrial history. It has been exceedingly difficult to decide what to leave out!

I hope that I have put in a wide enough cross-section of items to please everyone, and I also hope that you have as much fun discovering these unusual aspects of Staffordshire as Alan and I have had photographing and researching them.

Ros Prince

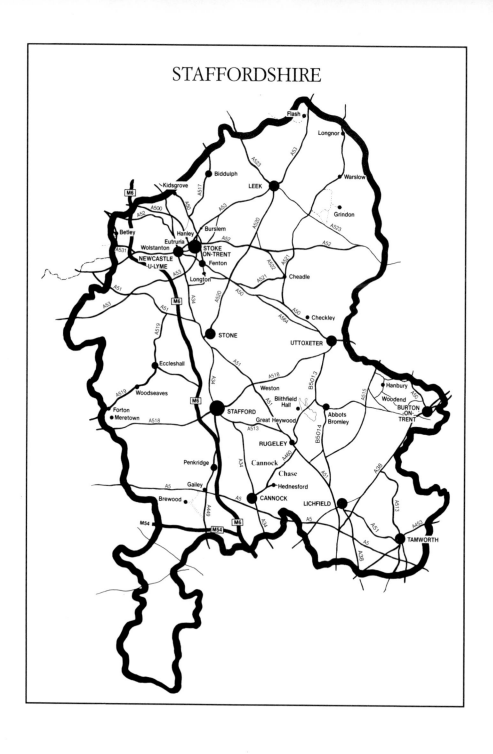

FLASH
THREE SHIRES HEAD

Access: Follow the A53 Leek to Buxton road, turn left at Axe Edge for Knotbury.

Map Reference: Ordnance Survey map 111 (1:50,000); SK 009 685.

Besides being the junction of three county boundaries, Staffordshire, Cheshire and Derbyshire, it is also the junction of four pack-horse routes, and incongruously, so great was the traffic concentrated in this otherwise sparsely populated area that the bridge had to be widened.

Within a very small area, three of the Moorlands rivers rise: the Dove, the Manifold and the Dane. A further two rivers rise over the border, the Wye and the Goyt. The Dove and the Manifold both have the curious habit of vanishing underground from time to time.

Nearby Panniers Pool was the scene of cock-fighting and bare-knuckle boxing when the area was frequented by the itinerant button sellers and peddlers from Manchester.

Names on the map should give you a good idea of the continuing wildness of the terrain in this area: Wolf Edge, Hawk's Nest, Wildboarclough, and Adders Green. Add to this wild and woolly atmosphere, a quantity of disused mine shafts and the sensible explorer will know to take extra care, and not to linger into dusk!

FLASH
THE VILLAGE

> *Access:* Follow the A53 Leek to Buxton road, turn left at the signpost for Flash.
> *Map Reference:* Ordnance Survey map 111 (1:50,000); SK 025 672.

The original name of this village was Quarnford, but it has been popularly called Flash for so long that the road signs now bear that name.

In previous centuries the village was the haunt of coiners. It is said that the conterfeit coins glittered, being much brighter than the real coins, and so became known as 'flash' money.

The 'industry' was centred here because of the village's close proximity to Three Shire Heads, where the boundaries of Staffordshire, Cheshire and Derbyshire meet, so if the constabulary or excise men were seen coming from one direction, the felons could skip over the appropriate boundary line, where the officers had no jurisdiction, and so escape apprehension!

Flash is the highest village in England, at 1500 feet, and though The New Inn provides a bright and welcoming atmosphere, it only needs a grey day to transport the imagination easily back to the bleak times when the village was literally a den of thieves.

THORNCLIFF
THE MERMAID

> *Access:* Take A53 Leek to Buxton road, turn right at the Moss Rose Inn and through to Thorncliff.
>
> *Map Reference:* Ordnance Survey map 111 (1:50,000); SK 036 604.

Why should a pub high on the moors in the middle of England bear the name of a mythical sea creature? Because, according to legend, The Mermaid lives in nearby Blakemere Pool and will drag unwary travellers to their doom in its dark depths.

This part of the Staffordshire Moorlands was very remote in the days of pack-horse trains and peddlers, and more than one was attacked travelling these lonely roads. But I think it would be less of the mermaid luring these wayfarers to their deaths, and more of the footpads and high-waymen who infested the area, getting rid of the evidence in some convenient water!

Whatever the threat, the jaggers, drovers and peddlers were glad to see the gleam of light from The Mermaid's windows in the gathering gloom, to remind them there were others alive on the moors.

THORNCLIFF
A RAMBLER REMEMBERED

Access: Take A53 Leek to Buxton road, turn right at the Moss Rose Inn and
through to Thorncliff. Park on the left before the Mermaid Inn.

Map Reference: Ordnance Survey map 111 (1:50,000); SK 028 597.

Despite being a world traveller Paul Rey must have especially loved the view from the
moorland road between Thorncliff and the Mermaid Inn. At a particularly splendid
vantage point a discreet stone monument has been erected to his memory.

It faces out towards the Roaches, the Cheshire Plain and the distant Welsh mountains, and
reads, 'To the memory of Paul Rey (1925-1977) a rambler and world traveller who
inspired so many with his love of the countryside.'

It also shows crow-flying distances to the various points of interest which can be seen from
there: Mow Cop—10¼ miles, Jodrell Bank—16 miles, Hen Cloud—1 mile, Roaches—
2¼ miles, and so on.

Regrettably, the useful seat beside the memorial stone attracts the litter droppers, so you
may have to gather up some chip papers and cigarette packets before you can appreciate
fully what Paul Rey so admired.

LONGNOR
A SCULPTOR'S MISTAKE

Access: Follow the A515 Buxton to Ashbourne road, then B5053 to Longnor.
Map Reference: Ordnance Survey map 111 (1:50,000); SK 089 650.

An interesting sculptor's mistake can be discovered on an epitaph wall of Longnor Church. It is located on the wall to the right of the entrance to the church, opposite Billy Billinge's grave (see page 6).

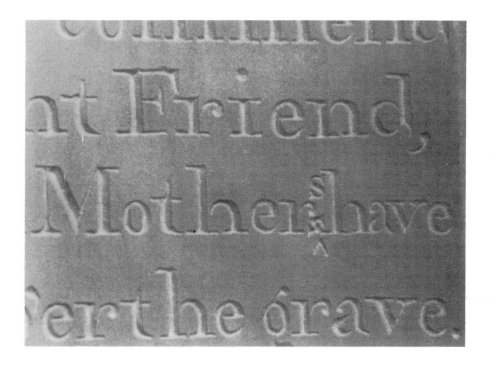

LONGNOR
BILLY BILLINGE — AN OLD SOLDIER

Access: Take A515 Buxton to Ashbourne road, then B5053 to Longnor.

Map Reference: Ordnance Survey map 111 (1:50,000); SK 089 650.

Staffordshire Moorlands dwellers have a reputation for hardiness — and longevity as well in some instances! William Billinge is a case in point. He lived to be 112 and died within 150 yards of the place where he had been born. His headstone in Longnor churchyard gives a potted biography of a busy life.

He was born in 1679 in a cornfield at Fawfieldhead, became a soldier at 23, and served under Sir George Rooke. He was at the taking of the fortress of Gibraltar in 1704, and was then in the service of the Duke of Marlborough at the Battle of Ramilles in 1706 where he was wounded by a musket ball. However, he fought again for the King in the Stuart rebellions of 1715 and 1745.

The original headstone had fallen into disrepair by the beginning of this century and was replaced by a facsimile in 1903. The money was raised by public subscription, the villagers being proud of their soldier hero whose exemplary actions in leading a group of soldiers to protect the fallen John Churchill had undoubtedly saved the Duke of Marlborough's life.

LONGNOR
MARKET TOLLS

> *Access:* Take A515 Buxton to Ashbourne road, then B5053 to Longnor.
> *Map Reference:* Ordnance Survey map 111 (1:50,000); SK 089 650.

The population of Longnor at the end of the 1980s was about 400, but in 1873, when the market hall was built, the sleepy village was a thriving market town of some 520 souls. It had no less than 7 shoemakers (people had to walk a lot!), 4 tailors and a milliner/dressmaker, and 5 grocers. There was also a horse-shoe maker, bakers, carpenters, a watchmaker, 2 butchers, saddle and harness makers, 2 druggists, the registrar and surveyor of turnpikes, the foot-postman and a cooper; everyone in fact to make a community virtually self-sufficient.

Markets were held on Tuesday, the day before nearby Leek. Things were always so arranged that market towns within walking distance of one another didn't compete for business on the same day. The list of tolls (below) to be paid by the market traders is still emblazoned on the front of the market hall (above), and reading through them it is easy to transport yourself back to Longnor's bustling past.

LONGNOR
WASHGATE BRIDGE

Access: From Longnor take the Hollinsclough road. On leaving Hollinsclough
take the footpath to the right.

Map Reference: Ordnance Survey map 111 (1:50,000); SK 061 670.

It is relatively rare to find a pack-horse bridge in original condition, but a charming example can be found in Washgate Bridge, which crosses the upper reaches of the Dove and therefore must have a foot in each of the counties of Staffordshire and Derbyshire.

Pack-horse bridges can be recognised by the fact that they have very low parapets or none at all, for the simple reason that high parapets would have caught the sides of the wide panniers of the packs and probably damaged the contents. There were enough breakages anyway. Most of the bridges were also constructed to be narrow, thus preventing the bridge being overloaded by too many ponies at once. They were therefore stronger and safer.

Many of these bridges on the old routes date from medieval times, but pack-horse bridges were still being constructed in the early nineteenth century.

GRINDON
A SNOWY SACRIFICE

> *Access:* From the Leek to Ashbourne road take B5053 to Warslow at Bottom House. After Onecote turn right for Grindon.
>
> *Map Reference:* Ordnance Survey map 111 (1:50,000); SK 085 546.

The spires of Butterton and Grindon churches are charming landmarks for ramblers during the summer months, but in the horrendous winter of 1947 they towered over a cold and hostile landscape, as snowbound villagers rapidly ran out of their stockpiled supplies. There seemed to be no alternative to a mercy flight by the R.A.F.

A successful food drop of some 20,000 lbs was made at Longnor, and on the morning of Thursday 13 February 1947 a Halifax and its crew flew over Grindon Moor, looking through the murk for a black cross of soot on the snow. As they approached it seemed that a wing tip caught the ground, and the Halifax crashed in a ball of flame killing all eight crew members before the eyes of the horrified villagers.

That day the road to Leek was opened up and supplies came in by road. An official report maintained the flight was necessary, but villagers were not convinced. They hadn't asked for help, sure that they and their neighbours could eke out supplies between them. They erected a memorial to the men in Grindon Church, listing their names 'In Grateful Remembrance'.

THE ROACHES
THE WINKING MAN

> *Access:* Best seen travelling to Buxton from Leek on A53. The rocks are on the left, just past Upper Hulme.
>
> *Map Reference:* Ordnance Survey map 111 (1:50,000); SK 020 623.

If you ever travel from Leek to Buxton, look out at the escarpment on the left. You will see the rough outline of a man's head appear, with a gap as an eye socket, and as you pass by he will wink at you! This is caused by rocks behind obscuring the gap for a moment.

The area behind is known as The Roaches, stemming from the French word for rocks, 'roches'. On a part of the Roaches lives a colony of wallabies, descendants of escapees from a private zoo several decades ago. The zoo belonged to Lt. Col. Brocklehurst who had been a game warden in the Sudan, and his collection included deer, a kangaroo, the wallabies, and yaks. Only the deer and wallabies remain, and are timid creatures best left undisturbed. Survival is hard enough for the wallabies with the severe Moorlands weather, though hopefully a succession of mild winters, and some generous farmers who put hay out for them, will have allowed the little colony, always on the verge of extinction, to build up its numbers.

LEEK
A DOUBLE SUNSET AND A VERY OLD MAN

> *Access:* On the A523 Macclesfield road, opposite its junction with the A53.
>
> *Map Reference:* Ordnance Survey map 110 (1:50,000); SJ 982 567.

From the vantage point of St Edward's churchyard in Leek at midsummer, 20 to 22 June, it is possible to watch the sun set twice. It disappears completely behind Bosley Cloud and then reappears to set again over the Cheshire Plain.

Weather conditions have to be right, of course, to be able to see this, but every year many hopefuls turn up to watch.

While you are in the churchyard, on the west side near the tower door, look for the gravestone for 'James Robinson interr'd February 28th 1788 aged 438'. Obviously the sculptor had got into the swing of putting an 8 at the end of every number, and his mind was probably on going home for his tea. I think Mr Robinson was only 43 — the 8 is a little less defined — time and money would, no doubt, preclude the provision of a correct stone — oops!

LEEK
THE NICHOLSON INSTITUTE

> *Access:* On the A523 Macclesfield road, just below the Council Offices in Stockwell Street.
>
> *Map Reference:* Ordnance Survey map 110 (1:50,000); SJ 983 567.

The green copper dome of the Nicholson Institute is a splendid landmark and tribute to Joshua Nicholson, who wanted to ensure that the good people of Leek had a cultural centre in the form of a public library, museum and art gallery, with rooms for art and science classes where the artisans could better themselves.

His ghost, or that of a former librarian, is said to lurk in the nether regions of the library, and has been spotted by members of staff in the past.

In 1965, Leek was set by the ears, and actually made the pages of the national press, with the discovery of what appeared to be the mummified remains of a child in the loft of the museum in the Institute. It was found by a painter during a bit of a tidy up! It was secreted in a barrel, but fortunately it turned out to be the carefully dissected body of an orang-utang. The date was 1 April, but this was a coincidence!

It is such a splendid building that the BBC used it to represent 'Bursley' Town Hall in one of their classical productions, Arnold Bennett's *The Old Wives' Tale* (broadcast as *Sophia and Constance*).

Many famous people visited the new Institute: Mark Twain, George Bernard Shaw, even George VI and Queen Mary when they were Duke and Duchess of York. The building was constructed as a showpiece and it is to the architects' credit that the lovely building in front of it, the recently renovated Greystones, was preserved even though it partly obscures their prestigious design.

LEEK
OAK TERRACE

Access: Take the A53 to Stoke-on-Trent. Oak Terrace is on the left leaving Leek.
Map Reference: Ordnance Survey map 110 (1:50,000); SJ 977 557.

This splendid terrace in Leek is an absolute joy, completely unadulterated, remaining exactly as the architect and builder intended.

All credit to the owners, none of whom have decided to dispense with a bay, alter apertures, or fit incompatible windows anywhere.

The terrace was constructed in 1916, right in the middle of the first world war, and so often, formerly handsome terraces of this age have been ruined by the application of stone cladding to one or two dwellings, or the removal of a feature destroying the original design. It is refreshing to see relatively humble housing treated with the same respect as a stately home. It gives me great pleasure to look at Oak Terrace as I go past, and I was delighted to see in August 1990 that it is intended that these buildings should be listed.

CHEADLE
LES'S 'OSS AND CART

Access: From Cheadle take the B5417 to Oakamoor. Situated on the right just outside Cheadle.

Map Reference: Ordnance Survey map 111 (1:50,000); SK 021 437.

Everyone in the Cheadle area knows Les Oakes, and many from an even wider area know of his farm, Hales View. When you see it you will know why! The farm bungalow is unprepossessing, but the farm buildings are a fabulous riot of cornices, mouldings and bits and bobs salvaged from demolished buildings around North Staffordshire and beyond.

Les does a grand job preserving these little works of art, incorporating them into an ongoing building programme to rival any of the eighteenth-century folly builders. The front wall of one has a nice brickwork picture proclaiming, Les's 'oss and cart — more delights are around every corner!

The buildings do serve a function though, as they house Les's collection of horse-drawn vehicles, memorabilia, street furniture, advertising signs and paraphernalia of every sort and description. You can buy all sorts of wood, doors, windows, sinks etc. The whole place, and Les, is a delight.

If you are lucky you can get special dispensation to see Les's private collection, housed in a labyrinth of lofts. It was formerly open to all, but is now closed to the general public because of petty pilfering.

Hales View Farm

Part of Les's private collection

NEWCASTLE-UNDER-LYME
THE NEWCASTLE REGICIDE

Access: In High Street, opposite the Guildhall.
Map Reference: Ordnance Survey map 110 (1:50,000); SJ 848 459.

A plaque on the wall of the Midland Bank in Newcastle's market-place recalls the name of John Bradshawe, a former recorder of the city and infamous as the chief prosecutor of King Charles I.

It was a dirty job and no one else wanted such a task, but Bradshawe was an ambitious man and a staunch supporter of Cromwell. John Bradshawe had little hesitation in putting his name first on the King's death warrant.

He was fulsomely paid for his services in getting rid of the rightful king and was one of Cromwell's closest friends. He died in 1659, just in time, as in 1660 Charles II was restored to the throne! The bodies of Cromwell, Ireton and Bradshawe were exhumed and hanged at Tyburn and then reburied ignominiously below the gallows, while their decomposing heads were exhibited on spikes in Westminster, so that all could jeer and witness the fate of traitors.

HANLEY
CITY MUSEUM AND ART GALLERY

Access: Park in the centre of Hanley. From the shopping area walk down
Piccadilly. The museum is situated opposite the junction with the main
road to Stoke. Signposted from the town centre.

Map Reference: Ordnance Survey map 110 (1:50,000); SJ 882 474.

The attractive frieze of Hanley museum depicts a variety of Potteries occupations, and the
inconspicuous heap of stones to the left of the entranceway is a direct link with the pottery
industry. It isn't a heap of rubble, but the foundations of an early kiln.

Inside is the reminder of another unique claim to fame: a Spitfire, Reginald Mitchell
having been born in the Potteries.

The Pottery Collection, as you would expect, is of world class. Students from far and wide
come to visit this.

The museum was opened in 1981 by the Prince of Wales, and was desperately needed. Six
times the size of the old museum which it replaced, it deservedly won the Museum of the
Year Award in 1982.

HANLEY
TELEPHONE BUILDINGS

Access: From the museum, cross the main road into Marsh Street. Situated at the second junction on the left-hand side.

Map Reference: Ordnance Survey map 110 (1:50,000); SJ 882 474.

Situated on the corner of Marsh Street and Trinity Street, this glorious example of Edwardian Renaissance was opened in 1900 to cope with the increasing demand for that modern wonder of communication, the telephone!

In 1890 there had been a mere 211 subscribers in the Potteries, but by 1904 there were over 2,000, and the National Telephone Company's directory covered the whole country.

This extremely solid and handsome building has recently been cleaned and restored and is a marvellous asset to the architectural history of the Potteries.

LONGTON
FOLEY PLACE

Access: Take A50 from Stoke to Longton. Situated on the right just before the
start of the one way system.

Map Reference: Ordnance Survey map 110 (1:50,000); SJ 905 439.

Watching the restoration of this row of houses, originally built in the 1850s for the
modestly prosperous residents of Longton, has provided a lot of pleasure for many people.
Add to that the fact that they have provided homes for families in urgent need, and I think
everyone will congratulate the Beth Johnson Foundation.

The Foundation has done its best to restore the Terrace from a derelict condition to the
original street scene, and there are now 7 two-bedroomed, three-storied residences.

Originally the terrace overlooked a garden, however, the location wasn't right to attract
the kind of residents for whom the development had been intended. It had been aimed at
the middle classes, with quarters for a servant; but they had been build adjacent to large
pottery factories, the main railway line, a mineral line, and a busy main road. In addition
the terrace formed an L with the Foley Arms public house! Tenancies changed frequently
(curiously in 1867, three of the houses were let to photographic artists) and it was obvious
from numerous vacant houses that the landlord was having difficulty attracting the kind
of residents he had wanted — but what desirable homes they are now!

LONGTON
THE GLADSTONE

Access: Take A50 from Stoke to Longton. Situated on the right after the end of the one way system in Longton.

Map Reference: Ordnance Survey map 110 (1:50,000); SJ 912 433.

Not a bag, but a museum to the pottery industry which was museum of the year in 1976. Here you can see four examples of the infamous bottle ovens which used to dominate the skyline throughout the Potteries, and which were demolished in such huge numbers when they became obsolete that they are now a great rarity. They certainly did their bit in polluting the Potteries!

The Gladstone is a complete Victorian potbank. China has been made on the site for 200 years, although the main building dates from 1856. It closed in the mid-sixties, having remained unmodernised, which is why it was so important to rescue it.

You can try some typical Potteries food here: lobby (a kind of stew) no use to vegetarians, and Trentham tart.

The Gladstone also houses the oldest telegraph pole in the country, donated by the post office in recognition of the signal service of the Potteries in providing the insulators.

BUCKNALL
A WELCOME DRINK

> *Access:* From the centre of Hanley take the Ashbourne road. Situated on the left just before the road becomes dual carriageway.
>
> *Map Reference:* Ordnance Survey map 110 (1:50,000); SJ 893 476.

On the corner of Bucknall Old Road and Bucknall New Road is a water trough which must have provided a refreshing drink for those, with two legs or four, who had just struggled up Lime Kiln Bank. It is bad enough driving up with plenty of horse power under the bonnet, but with only a couple of horses' power, and pulling a loaded cart behind you, it must have made some tongues hang out, until they reached this trough.

Usually these watering points would have some sort of cup or ladle attached to them to enable the driver to have a drink too, and indeed the inscription reads:

'TO MAN AND BEAST. ALL AKIN. G. WEDGWOOD. 1879'.

It was presented to the Borough of Hanley in 1879.

STOKE-UPON-TRENT
A JACOBEAN STATION

Access: Follow the Station signs from the D-road (A500) or any main road into the city.

Map Reference: Ordnance Survey map 110 (1:50,000); SJ 880 457.

Stoke station was originally designed as one side of what was intended to be the Potteries main town square. Pevsner describes it as . . . 'the finest piece of Victorian axial planning in the country'. It must be viewed in conjunction with the North Stafford Hotel opposite, which could easily be taken to have started life as an early Jacobean mansion. Railway offices completed the north and south sides of the design.

The entrance to the station is through a round arched Tuscan colonnade and the facade had three gables. It was built for the North Staffs. Railway Company, later known with affection as The Knotty, and as their boardroom was on the first floor it had a splendid window of eight lights incorporated into the design to illuminate the worthies within.

The station was opened in 1848, and the hotel a year later. The whole scheme is executed in dark red local brick, with the patterns picked out in Staffordshire blue brick. A very impressive square.

ETRURIA
SHIRLEY'S BONE MILL

> *Access:* From Hanley follow the signs for Festival Park. Turn left at the Festival roundabout and situated several hundred yards on the right — signposted Etruria Industrial Museum.
>
> *Map Reference:* Ordnance Survey map 110 (1:50,000); SJ 872 468.

Yes, I'm afraid bone china does have bones in it, and Jesse Shirley had the Etruscan Bone and Flint Mill erected in Etruria, by the canal in 1857, to process flint and bone for supplying the pottery industry.

It is a two-storey building with a drying kiln for bones and flints at one end, and at the other an engine-house which is home to Princess — a beautiful beam engine.

Why flint was originally used in pottery making is a mystery. There is a school of thought which attributes it to Thomas Astbury of Shelton, who was amazed at the fineness of the ground flint which he saw an ostler packing into a horse's eye to treat New Forest disease. The Welsh use ground slate for the same purpose, so if Mr Astbury had visited Blaenau Ffestiniog instead of Dunstable, would we have had Shirley's bone and slate mill?

KIDSGROVE
THE HARECASTLE TUNNEL

Access: From the A500 D-road at the A34 roundabout, follow the signs for
Tunstall. After approximately one mile, park on the right after a sharp
bend immediately after a junction (small gravel parking area only).
Walk down the path to the lock-keeper's cottage. The canal is not
easily visible from the road without leaving your car.
Map Reference: Ordnance Survey map 110 (1:50,000); SJ 849 518.

Driving a tunnel through Harecastle Hill presented so many problems that some people
dismissed it as another of Brindley's 'Air Castles', but he carried on imperviously.

It is about 3,000 yards long and took 11 years to dig. There is no towpath, the horses had to
be taken over the hill to the other side and the bargees legged the boats through by lying
on their backs and walking along the roof. It was opened in 1777, and the first Kidsgrove
residents were the Navigators who had camped at that end of the tunnel during its
construction.

Increasing use of the canals highlighted a bottleneck at Harecastle. In 1827 another tunnel,
engineered by Telford beside the first, was opened having taken only three years to
complete due to improvements in tunnelling technique, a supply of skilled workmen and
an even greater supply of funds from the new prosperous canal company. The original
tunnel is closed, but Telford's is back in use.

BURSLEM
A WITCHES' GRAVE

Access: From Hanley go through Cobridge following the signs for Burslem. St John's Church is situated in one of the many side streets to the left of the main road, close to the centre of Burslem.
Map Reference: Ordnance Survey map 110 (1:50,000); SJ 864 495.

In the cemetery of St John's Church, Burslem, there is a grave turned on a north-south axis, therefore at right angles to all the other graves. It is the grave of Margaret (or Molly, or Peggy) Leigh, who had a reputation for witchcraft. She lived at Jackfield, in the Hamil area, and was originally buried, on 1 April 1748, in the normal east-west alignment. However, when the burial party returned they discovered the lady sitting in her usual place in the chimney corner doing her knitting!

The parson, who reputedly liked a tipple, undertook to return to the churchyard with bell, book and candle (to lay the ghost), some other clergymen (for moral support) and his sexton and clerk (to do the digging). In the event the other clergymen ran off in a panic and there were only three left to realign her. They layed her back 'in the shape of a blackbird', whatever that might be. Some sources maintain that a live blackbird was put in the coffin with her.

Her mother died 20 years later and was buried in the same grave and in the same alignment.

WOLSTANTON
AN ACCUSATORY EPITAPH

Access: From the A500 D-road follow the Wolstanton signs. The church is on the left in the centre of Wolstanton.
From Newcastle follow the signs for The Brampton at the roundabout at the end of Ironmarket. Wolstanton is approximately 1½ miles further on.
Map Reference: Ordnance Survey map 110 (1:50,000); SJ 847 509.

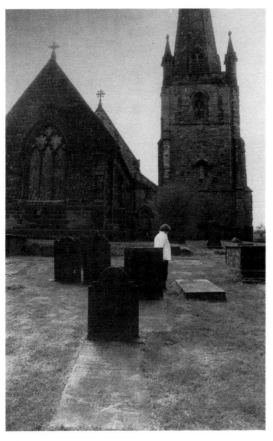

St Margaret's Church, Wolstanton, Nr. Newcastle has a most interesting epitaph, which in the present age would no doubt provoke some serious litigation!

It is on the grave of Sarah Smith, aged 21, who died on 29 November 1763 and it reads:

It was G-S B-W
that brought me to my end
dear parents mourn not for me
for God will stand my friend.
With half a pint of poyson
He came to visit me.
Write this on my grave
that all that read it may see

BETLEY
ST MARGARET'S CHURCH AND THE VILLAGE

> *Access:* From Newcastle follow the signs for Madeley. Stay on the main road
> at Madeley Heath (A531) and follow the signs for Betley.
> *Map Reference:* Ordnance Survey map 110 (1:50,000); SJ 756 484.

St Margaret's Church is of considerable interest here. It has a nave dating from about 1285
and an attractive timbered north porch, but the most interesting feature to me is the
timber arcading, which is made of whole tree trunks.

The wood is Spanish chestnut and each pillar is octagonal, but all is not what it seems! —
the centre of each is now concrete — a necessity caused by the depredations of the death-
watch beetle.

Betley village has a number of half-timbered buildings and was a thriving market town
until the end of the nineteenth century, and until the second world war three large estates
completely surrounded the village: Betley Old Hall, Betley Court, and Betley Hall. The
latter was demolished in the last war but there still exists the lake upon which Florence
Nightingale spent many happy hours boating.

MUCKLESTONE
THE BATTLE OF BLORE HEATH

Access: From Newcastle follow the signs for Market Drayton (A53).
Map Reference: Ordnance Survey map 110 (1:50,000); SJ 725 373.

The War of the Roses, fought between the royal houses of York and Lancaster, was the reason for the bloodiest battle ever fought in Staffordshire. The Battle of Blore Heath was contested by 10,000 Lancastrian supporters, led by Lord Audley, and 5,000 Yorkists following the Earl of Salisbury to Ludlow. The five-hour confrontation resulted in victory for the smaller 'white rose' army. More than 2,400 were killed, causing (it is said) the stream to run blood-red for days. Among the dead was Lord Audley himself, killed by Sir Roger Kynaston.

A wooden cross was originally erected on the field of battle to mark the spot where Audley fell. A stone cross replaced the original in 1765 on the orders of the Lord of the Manor, Charles Boothby Skrimsher. It can be found in a field on the left of the main road (A53) approximately 1¼ miles west of Loggerheads.

An interesting story claims that Queen Margaret, wife of Henry VI, watched the defeat of her army from the tower of Mucklestone Church. In order to make good her escape and to avoid capture, she had the shoes of her horse reversed by local blacksmith, William Skelhorn, and fled to Eccleshall castle. The plaque shown in the photograph was erected on the site of his former smithy to commemorate the work of the queen's loyal servant. It is located on the front of the house opposite the church. Notice also William Skelhorn's anvil in the churchyard opposite the plaque.

CHECKLEY
CHECKLEY CHURCH

Access: When leaving Uttoxeter, take the A522 Cheadle road. After travelling
approximately five miles, the church is on the left.

Map Reference: Ordnance Survey map 120 (1:50,000); SK 028 379.

The whole of Checkley is a very historic area and the church has many interesting features,
not least the ghost of an old lady who wanders in the graveyard.

On the bench ends of the choir stalls, there are carvings of Red Indians dating from the
sixteenth century — not long after the discovery of America, but why they are in Checkley
is a mystery.

Outside, the many grooves in the chancel buttresses are caused by archers sharpening their
arrows there. In the churchyard are three Saxon cross shafts. One of them is reputed to
commemorate the death of three bishops, who lost their lives in a major battle between
the Danes and Saxons at nearby Deadman's Green. This was so named because of the
number of casualties from the encounter who lie buried there (one of the field names here
is Top Naked Field because the warriors fought naked). The crosses are older than the
church building, but the churchyard probably predates them.

The church also has some sixteenth-century glass roundels which could be of Dutch
origin. They are supposed to have come from Rectory Farm, another interesting building
with some ancient features situated at the end of Church Lane.

ABBOTS BROMLEY
THE ABBOTS BROMLEY HORN DANCE

Access: Take the A518 Stafford road from Uttoxeter. Turn left on to the
B5013 to Abbots Bromley one mile outside Uttoxeter.
Map Reference: Ordnance Survey map 120 (1:50,000); SK 084 244

This could be the oldest surviving ceremony in Britain. Certainly one set of antlers carried by the dancers has been carbon dated to about 1000 BC, when Abbots Bromley was owned by Wulfric Spot. It is fairly safe to assume that the ritual predates the Norman conquest.

The dance always takes place on the Monday after the Sunday following 4 September. At 8.30 am the dancers fetch their reindeer horns, which are kept in the church, and the first dance takes place on the vicarage lawn.

There are six horndancers, wearing costume which looks vaguely Elizabethan. This practice only dates from the 1880s, at the instigation of a vicar's wife. Prior to that, the dancers had always worn their own clothes bedecked with ribbons. The horns, which vary in weight from 16 to 25 lbs, are attached to wooden reindeer heads which appear to be of sixteenth-century origin. They rest on the dancers' shoulders — a necessity as the dance takes all day and travels all round the village. If by ill chance a farm was to be missed out, bad luck would be sure to befall the inhabitants!

The dancers return to the village as dusk falls having stopped for lunch at Blithfield Hall. It makes a very arduous day, but obviously an honour to be prized. The same families tend to provide the dancers for generations; one family is reputed to have taken part for the last 400 years.

Besides the dancers who carry the horns, there is Maid Marion (a man in female medieval costume who carries an old wooden ladle), a hobby horse with clacking jaws, a boy who carries a bow with arrow attached and a fool in the conventional fool's garb. There are also two musicians, one with a triangle and one with an accordion, the hobby horse clacking time with its jaws and Maid Marion banging the ladle with a stick!

The original ceremony was performed at New Year and on Twelfth Day but was banned by the puritans after the civil wars. It had been revived by the early-eighteenth century and presumably that was when it began to be performed on Wakes Monday.

There are several theories as to the reasons for its existence. Most connect it to Abbots Bromley's close proximity to Needwood Forest. A charter of 1125 gave forest hunting rights to the villagers (who, no doubt, from time immemorial depended on the forest for their venison). So it could be a foresters' dance, or a dance to invoke magic to protect the hunters and ensure success in the chase. Whatever its origins, to see this ancient rite performed in the gathering dusk, as they dance their way back to the church, can be an eerie experience.

Abbots Bromley Horn Dance

BLITHFIELD HALL
BAGOT'S GOATS

Access: Leave Abbots Bromley towards Uttoxeter, take left turn for Rugeley (B5013), then first right down the private road.
Map Reference: Ordnance Survey map 110 (1:50,000); SK 081 264.

Blithfield Hall was built as the ancestral residence of the noble family of Bagot. It was also home to their distinctive goats, which are now in the charge of the Rare Breeds Society. The goats were supposedly brought back to this country by returning crusaders, and were given to the Bagots in thanks for a good day's hunting. It has been said by 'They Who Do Not Like The Goats', that the particular crusaders must have had a very poor day's hunting, because you don't give away goats you like, do you?

The goat theme is carried through to Goat Lodge, which was designed by Trubshaw in 1839 as an entrance lodge. It is more of a folly, as it was not very practical to live in. It is an attractive confection, now subtly extended so that the new building does not interfere with the original design. The chimneys are ornamented with deers' heads and the gables are beautifully bargeboarded, but the part from which it derives its name is the porchway which has a row of goats heads scowling down at visitors.

Goat Lodge

HANBURY
ST WERBURGH'S CHURCH

Access: From the A50 Uttoxeter-Derby road, take the A515 Lichfield road at
Sudbury. After two miles turn left for Hanbury.

Map Reference: Ordnance Survey map 120 (1:50,000); SK 071 279.

In the seventh century a priory existed at Hanbury. It was founded by King Ethelred of
Mercia, whose niece, Werburgha, was prioress. She was eventually canonized, and pilgrims
flocked to her tomb; but fearful of Danish desecration, her remains were removed to
Chester, and indeed the priory did fall victim to Danish attack in AD 875.

St Werburgh's Church is interesting for having the oldest alabaster effigy in the county,
perhaps even the country. It is almost certainly of the local alabaster from Fauld, and is of
Sir John de Hanbury, who died in 1303.

The church also contains the tomb of Sir John Egerton, who died in 1662. He must have
been a staunch Royalist during the Civil Wars, as his sister insisted on his burial being at
the east end of the north aisle, . . . so that he might be away from the gaze of the Puritan
ladies . . .

The Puritan ladies in question were Mrs Agarde, who died in 1628, and her daughter Mrs
Woollocke, who died in 1657. Their busts, in identical style and looking a trifle frowsty,
keep a disapproving eye on activities, and surely would have despised Sir John's flowing
locks and bucket-top boots!

Alabaster effigy of Sir John de Hanbury

FAULD
THE FAULD EXPLOSION

Access: Park in Hanbury (see previous item). Take the footpath on the left, just outside the village on the road to Woodend.

Map Reference: Ordnance Survey map 120 (1:50,000); SK 182 278.

Before the atomic bombs were dropped on Hiroshima and Nagasaki, the tiny village of Fauld had experienced the largest single explosion of the second world war, at 11.10am on Monday 27 November 1944. When part of the store of explosives in Ford's gypsum mines had gone up — about 7 million pounds of it — it took with it 81 people, countless farm animals and two woods. Upper Hayes Farm, directly over the mine, completely disappeared, and Hanbury Fields Farm was buried under the debris. The reservoir on the hill above the works breached and sent a vast wave of mud and debris over the plaster works, in some places to a depth of more than 15 feet.

Naked trees stood silhouetted against the sky. The ground was pitted with bomb craters. Bits of dead animals stuck up out of the ground in and around a huge crater which was 800 feet long, 300 feet wide and 120 feet deep. It was estimated that three million cubic yards of earth and rock had been thrown up and deposited over an area of a square mile around the crater.

The explosion damaged buildings up to ten miles away. People in Stoke, Leicester, Birmingham and Coventry heard it, and a seismograph in West Bromwich registered tremors for some minutes after the initial explosion. It was also recorded on seismographs in Geneva and Rome.

The miracle was that not all the explosives went up, since the two storage areas were separated by only a narrow connecting passageway. The total stock was about 15,000 tons, equivalent to a 15 kiloton nuclear device; and if all that had gone, so would Tutbury and other neighbouring villages.

To the villagers of Fauld and Hanbury, this is a grave site, and they would appreciate it if it was respected as such.

The dedication of the memorial stone erected in 1990.

ROCESTER
THE FOSSER

Access: From Uttoxeter follow the signs to Rocester and Alton Towers. The Fosser is on the right, opposite JCB factory.

Map Reference: Ordnance Survey map 120 (1:50,000); SK 107 396.

I must admit that factory sites are normally anathema to me, but the JCB factory at Rocester is in the most beautiful landscape, created with the lavish use of the firm's famous earth-moving equipment. It is all a world away from the company's humble beginnings: in the stable block of nearby Crakemarsh Hall, and a lock-up garage in Uttoxeter.

Three lakes provide a large expanse of water, always an attraction to the human species, as well as a large variety of water fowl. There are 35 breeds of ducks and geese here. The ornamentation is quite inspired too: a beautiful flock of metal birds takes off across a lake, and opposite, The Fosser stands sentinel on a mound.

This sculpture was designed by leading sculptor Walenty Pytel, constructed during the late seventies, and is made entirely of JCB machine parts.

Most of this landscaping is in public view, to be enjoyed for free. A bit which isn't, designed by Clifton Nurseries, and which has won the Award for Merit in the 1989 National Landscape Awards, is a formal French roof garden, with two fountains and various levels of illumination — but you have to wangle an invitation to see that!

ROCESTER
CRAKEMARSH HALL

> *Access:* From the A50 Uttoxeter bypass, take the B5053 for Rocester. The hall
> is on the left, 2 miles outside Uttoxeter.
>
> *Map Reference:* Ordnance Survey map 120 (1:50,000); SK 094 365.

The new Uttoxeter—Rocester bypass now travels in front of the gutted ruins of
Crakemarsh Hall, previously hidden away in its own grounds.

The present building dates from the first quarter of the nineteenth century and was rebuilt
round a splendid seventeenth-century staircase (later removed in the 1970s). It is very
reminiscent of the beautiful staircase in nearby Sudbury Hall. Crakemarsh is probably the
site of The Grange of Leys, which belonged to Croxden Abbey (certainly there are
Norman foundations in the cellars) and Bertram de Verdun had a place of devotion at
Crakemarsh; so 1,000 years of continuous occupation is now at an end.

It was formerly the home of the Cavendish family, one of whom unfortunately went down
on the *Titanic*. The portrait of a member of the family who had particularly loved
Crakemarsh was left hanging in the empty entrance hall when the last Cavendish left,
because there was a curse upon it. This was that ill-luck should befall whoever removed the
portrait as long as a wall of Crakemarsh stood. It was cut from its frame and stolen from
the empty house! I wonder if ill-luck dogged the culprit thereafter?

To the west of the hall ran the Uttoxeter spur of the old Caldon Canal which thus passed
between Crakemarsh and the private house now known as Lowfields. In the heyday of the
canals this house was a bargees' inn known as The Bug and Fiddle. Whether this was a
reference to the inhabitants of the bedlinen and the honesty of the landlord, or in
recognition of some talented insects we don't know, but I've always thought such a
wonderful name should be recorded for posterity!

BURTON-ON-TRENT — BASS MUSEUM
ROLL OUT THE BARREL . . .

Access: From Uttoxeter follow the A50 to Burton-on-Trent, then follow the signs to the Bass Museum.

Map Reference: Ordnance Survey map 120 (1:50,000); SK 247 235.

. . . or roll down the barrel in the case of the unique fountain at the Bass Brewery site in Burton. It was the brain-child of the Bass Engineers Department who also made it.

The structure utilises redundant metal beer casks and uses recycled water. As you can see from the photograph supplied by Circle Photography of Ansty, the fountain is particularly spectacular when there's some frost about.

UTTOXETER
DOCTOR JOHNSON WAS A NAUGHTY BOY

> *Access:* Drive into the centre of Uttoxeter. The kiosk is by the main road in the market-place.
>
> *Map Reference:* Ordnance Survey map 120 (1:50,000); SK 092 334.

In the market place in Uttoxeter is a kiosk from which a newspaper seller operates. Closer inspection shows it to be a memorial to the provider of our standard English Dictionary, who stood in Uttoxeter market place as a penance. I suppose many market stall holders have the same feeling on a cold, wet, winter's Wednesday!

However, our good Doctor was salving his conscience for having disobeyed his father, a bookseller. He had wanted his son to accompany him on the journey from Lichfield to Uttoxeter and to help out on the family stall at the market.

Johnson had refused, but his conscience had bothered him for the whole of his life, so when he was middle-aged he decided to expiate his sins by standing where he should have done 50 years previously.

UTTOXETER
A WELL-OILED CLOCKMAKER

Access: The church is in the centre of Uttoxeter, and is visible from the market square.

Map Reference: Ordnance Survey map 120 (1:50,000); SK 094 335.

As you can see from the picture, if some enterprising person had not recorded this inspired epitaph, it would have been lost to us long since.

It is in St Mary's Church, Uttoxeter, fourth stone on the left as you go through the gate and difficult to spot. My thanks to Jack Staley, the verger, for scrubbing the stone for me!

The epitaph is to a young 19-year-old watch-and-clock-maker of High St Uttoxeter, who obviously enjoyed many a tipple in his short life and cultivated some humorous cronies, if the verse is anything to go by. His young wife must have had a sense of humour too, as she joined her husband a few short years after and lies beneath the same stone.

The epitaph reads:

> *Here lies one who strove to equal time,*
> *A task too hard, each power too sublime,*
> *Time stopped his motion, o'erthrew his balance wheel,*
> *Wore off his pivots, though made of hardened steel;*
> *Broke all his springs, the verge of life decayed*
> *And now he is as though he'd ne'er been made.*
> *Not for the want of oiling, that he tried;*
> *If that had done, why then he'd ne'er have died.*

He was Joseph Slater who stopped ticking in 1822.

ELFORD
DEATH BY TENNIS

Access: From Tamworth take the A513 Alrewas road. Turn right into the
village, then left again for the church.

Map Reference: Ordnance Survey map 120 (1:50,000); SK 185 106.

There are many ways of quitting this life, but I should think one of the more bizarre is
being hit by a tennis ball. This unfortunate incident did occur in 1460 however, and just
goes to show that tennis balls are no longer what they were.

The memorial to John Stanley, the unhappy recipient of this mortal blow is in St Peter's
Church, Elford. He lies holding the offending tennis ball in his left hand, whilst pointing
with his right hand to his right temple. He looks fairly dispassionate about it all
though.

Besides this unusual memorial St Peter's is also justifiably renowned for its marvellous
collection of shields of the Lords of the Manor. All are in fine condition and date back to
Saxon times; and the effigy of Richard III's cousin, Lady Isabella Neville, is here too.

LICHFIELD
THE LADIES OF THE VALE

Access: Park in the centre of the city, or possibly in The Close itself, adjacent to the cathedral.

Map Reference: Ordnance Survey map 120 (1:50,000); SK 118 097.

What a lovely way to describe the three elegant spires of Lichfield Cathedral! Small, but beautifully set between Minster and Stowe Pools, it was damaged more than any other of our cathedrals during the Civil War. The central spire collapsed completely into the choir in 1646, and the Parliamentary soldiers stabled their horses inside.

Most of the cathedral which can be seen today is heavily Victorianised by Sir George Gilbert Scott and John Oldrid Scott, who finished restoration work in 1901.

Inside there are also two young ladies worth seeing — a memorial known as the sleeping children. It is to the Robinson children, made by Sir Francis Chantry, and must be the most popular monument in the cathedral. It is a sculpture in white marble and is positively Victorian in its sentimentality, but actually dates from 1814.

Sir Francis is reputed to have been so pleased with this particular work that he returned to it annually for inspiration.

LICHFIELD
DUMB DYOTT

Access: Leaving the cathedral main entrance, turn left into The Close then first right. The plaque is on Brooke House, just past the end of the Minster Pool.

Map Reference: Ordnance Survey map 120 (1:50,000); SK 117 096.

The story of Dumb Dyott has always been a favourite of mine since my schooldays in Lichfield. During the siege of the cathedral and the wrong but romantic Royalists by the right but repulsive Parliamentarians, a young man, brother of Sir Richard Dyott, and unfortunately deaf and dumb (hence his nickname) was on duty with two others on the cathedral roof watching the activities of the besiegers below.

Lord Brooke was in command of the Parliamentary force and emerged into the street to see how things did. He was very obvious, with a particularly distinctive steel helmet with plumes, and five gilt steel bars down the front. He raised his visor, the better to examine the enemy, and Dumb Dyott, undistracted by any extraneous sounds, raised his musket and fired, shooting Lord Brooke, through his right eye!

Many have claimed Divine Intervention, and considering the dubious accuracy of the Civil War musket, they may have a point. There is a plaque on a wall in Dam Street which marks the spot where Lord Brooke fell.

LICHFIELD
THE CAPTAIN OF THE *TITANIC*

> *Access:* Leave the cathedral main entrance. Go down the narrow road directly ahead. Cross the main road into Beacon Park.
>
> *Map Reference:* Ordnance Survey map 120 (1:50,000); SK 117 096.

Commander Edward John Smith, RD, RNR, was born in Hanley and was a very brave man, who went down with his ship the *Titanic*. The people of his birthplace didn't wish to acknowledge him and it was left to Lichfield to become home to his statue.

This stands in Beacon Park. Made of bronze, 7' 8" high on a plinth of Cornish granite, it was sculpted by Lady Kathleen Scott, the widow of the Antarctic explorer Captain Robert Falcon Scott.

Captain Smith's daughter Helen unveiled the statue on 29 July 1914, in the presence of Lady Scott. The simple memorial plaque reads: 'Cdr. Edward John Smith, RD, RNR, born 27th Jan 1850, Died 1st April 1912. Bequeathing to his countrymen the memory and example of a great heart, a brave life and a heroic death Be British.'

LICHFIELD
ST JOHN'S HOSPITAL

Access: From the cathedral travel towards Tamworth. The hospital is at the
major road junction by the railway station.

Map Reference: Ordnance Survey map 120 (1:50,000); SK 117 092.

The striking range of eight uniform chimney breasts fronting on to St John's Street cannot
be ignored. They belong to the eastern wall of St John's hospital, which was founded by
Bishop Roger de Clinton around 1140. Some of this original building still survives in the
south wall of the chapel and the north wall of the chapel range.

In 1495 the hospital was refounded by Bishop Smyth, and it is to this period that the
impressive range of chimney breasts seems to belong.

There is a tablet over the door dated 1720, but obviously much of the building is of earlier
date and there are also some additions from the twentieth century.

TAMWORTH
ST EDITHA'S STAIRCASE

> *Access:* St Editha's church is in the centre of the town, next to the market.
>
> *Map Reference:* Ordnance Survey map 120 (1:50,000); SK 207 041.

The parish church of St Editha, in Tamworth, is one of the county's largest and has a square tower with a spire at each corner. Although this is not too rare, one of these towers contains a crafty little arrangement of staircases, an idea illustrated by Leonardo da Vinci.

The entrance to one staircase is from the churchyard, and the other from the inside, so the floor of one forms the roof of the other. Thus the goers-up on one never see the comers-down on the other. Oddly, one has 106 steps and the other 101 (not that I have been up and counted, because spiral staircases give me hysterics).

There is a similar staircase in the Chateau of Chambard in France, and two more British ones at Much Wenlock and Pontefract.

SMALLRICE, NEAR SANDON
SMALLRICE GIN

Access: From Hilderstone (three miles east of Stone) travel south on the
B5066. Turn left at the sign for Smallrice, one mile before Sandon.
The farm is first right along the lane.

Map Reference: Ordnance Survey map 110 (1:50,000); SJ 952 316.

Horse power can be utilised in many ways, and Smallrice Farm, part of the Sandon Estate,
has an unusual adaptation for Staffordshire in the form of a horse gin. These are still quite
common in the north of the country, where they are known as gin gangs, but rare in the
midlands and further south.

The gin consisted of a circular building in which a horse was attached to an arm fixed in the
centre of the little building. The horse walked round and round, and thus drove machinery
in other farm buildings.

Meaford Hall Farm, Meaford, has a similar gin.

STONE
SCOTCH BROOK

Access: Take the A520 Longton road out of Stone. After two miles turn right for Moddershall. The mill is on the left.

Map Reference: Ordnance Survey map 110 (1:50,000); SJ 920 366.

The Scotch Brook runs from Moddershall to Stone through some breathtakingly dramatic scenery, and in so doing, in just three miles, provided the motive power for at least nine mills, most of which still survive in various states of repair.

It is believed that there was a corn mill in the Moddershall Valley in the twelfth century, and many of the mills were still working in the 1930s.

Ivy Mill is well preserved, a Grade II-listed building, and Mosty Lee Mill has been restored. It was built in 1716 as a fulling mill, converted to flint grinding in 1756, and was finally closed in 1958. It is situated on a notoriously dangerous stretch of the A520 just north of Stone, so take care if you are looking for it.

STONE
THE MUDLEYS

Access: From the centre of Stone, pass the railway station and leave Stone
towards Meaford. The Mudleys are on the right, on the outskirts of
Stone.

Map Reference: Ordnance Survey map 110 (1:50,000); SJ 897 352.

All the children of Stone must have played on The Mudleys at some point in their young
lives. The map shows it as a common plot, Mudley Pits, which is a corruption of Motley
Pits. Now it is just pitted, pock-marked, humpy terrain, the haunt of dog-walkers and
children, but on 3 December 1745 it saw a hasty gathering of the Duke of Cumberland's
army, mustering to face Bonny Prince Charlie at the head of some six or seven thousand
supporters, who seemed to be heading towards Stone from the north.

The artillery was drawn up on The Mudleys and the mounds and heaps were thrown up to
mount the cannons as high as possible for maximum range. Many of the soldiers were
housed in tents on the Stone Fields, with others billeted in the town.

There were three battalions of Cumberland's guards, eleven battalions of foot, and six
regiments of horse and dragoons. Bonnie Prince Charlie left Leek for Derby, not Stone,
with the result that there was no confrontation on The Mudleys. The army took off after
Bonnie Prince Charlie and the final battle eventually took place at Culloden.

STONE
ESCAPEES AT THE CROWN

Access: In the centre of Stone, halfway down High Street.
Map Reference: Ordnance Survey map 110 (1:50,000); SJ 902 339.

In 1745 the Stone Parish Constable managed to apprehend Richard Vaughan, one of Bonnie Prince Charlie's staff, who was trying to make his escape into Wales by crossing the Trent at Darlaston. He was taken to the Crown Hotel in the centre of Stone and detained there.

Shortly afterwards a gentleman arrived and wished to interview the rebel. He was duly taken through to the prisoner and left to his interrogation. After some considerable time the gentleman had still not emerged and someone went to investigate, only to discover that the gentleman and Sir Richard had vanished!

A less fortunate escapee was a poor pig which had made a bid for freedom from Stone Market. The terrified animal had bolted as far as the steps of The Crown, only to be stopped by the august personage of Sir Harry Secombe, a resident at the hotel, who thereby demonstrated that he can indeed stop a pig in an entry.

WOODSEAVES
THE SMALLEST TELEGRAPH POLE

> *Access:* Between Eccleshall and Newport, one mile south-west of Woodseaves. Situated under the road bridge over the canal and visible from the towpath.
>
> *Map Reference:* Ordnance Survey map 119 (1:50,000); SJ 789 242.

The ordinary traveller would never know this was here, tucked away as it is right beneath the bridge. The wood nearby, known as Ladywood, is said to be haunted because of a suicide committed there. Loynton Moss, the nature reserve, was once the site of Blakemere Pool, which has dried up and vanished from the map.

TITTENSOR
TITTENSOR MONUMENT

Access: Visible from the main A34 dual carriageway from Stone to Newcastle. Situated on the left just north of Tittensor.

Map Reference: Ordnance Survey map 110 (1:50,000); SJ 871 389.

More correctly it is The Sutherland Monument as it is to the first Duke of Sutherland, who before his elevation had been plain old George Granville Leveson-Gower of Trentham.

The design of the monument is by Winks. It was sculpted by Chantry and erected in 1834. The Duke was highly thought of by the populace; the inscription lauds his many virtues and concludes — 'a mourning and grateful tenantry uniting with the inhabitants of the neighbourhood erected this pillar'. The Duke stands adopting a classical pose on a stone column, which itself stands on a tiered pedestal.

There is a local expression which derives from this monument to the good Duke. When you wish to galvanize someone into action who is idling about with apparently little to do, you say to them . . . come on, shape yourself, yer standin' about like Tittensor Monument! . . .

CANNOCK CHASE
A GERMAN CEMETERY

Access: From Cannock follow the A34 north towards Stafford. The cemetery is signposted on the right approximately three miles from the centre of Cannock.

Map Reference: Ordnance Survey map 119 (1:50,000); SJ 983 155.

Cannock Chase consists of some 30,000 acres of uplands and moors, the remains of the famous Royal Forest.

Tucked away against the woods close to the Cank Thorn is the German Military Cemetery, and close by, the Commonwealth Cemetery. Maintained by the War Graves Commission they are a memorial to those who died far away from their homes.

The Commonwealth Cemetery contains the graves of many New Zealanders who died in the influenza epidemic at the end of the first world war, and in the German Cemetery lie 5,000 soldiers killed in the two world wars, including the crews of four Zeppelins brought down during 1916/17. The Hall of Remembrance was designed by Professor Diez Brandt.

CANNOCK CHASE
CANK THORN

Access: From the German Cemetery entrance the bush is situated immediately across the road.

Map Reference: Ordnance Survey map 119 (1:50,000); SJ 983 155.

You could be forgiven for thinking that a thorn bush is a thorn bush — but some thorn bushes are more important than other thorn bushes! Take, for example, The Cank Thorn. This is a very special bush, the rooted sucker taken from the old stock of a previous bush growing on this exact spot as bushes have grown here for at least 600 years.

Since time immemorial thorn bushes have been used to mark boundaries, and this one marks the edge of Cannock Chase. This is also the meeting place of the three ancient manors of Rugeley, Penkridge and Cannock, and so despite its innocuous appearance, it is a very important little bush!

CANNOCK CHASE
CASTLE RING

Access: Approximately four miles south of Rugeley and east of Cannock. Signposted from both towns.

Map Reference: Ordnance Survey map 120 (1:50,000); SK 045 126.

This is a magnificent hill fort situated some 800 feet up on the highest point of Cannock Chase, and is in an excellent defensive position. It is the largest of the seven hill forts situated in the county, and really one of the best in the whole country, extending over about nine acres.

The south side being the weakest, the fort is defended here by no less than five lines of ramparts, and on the less vulnerable sides by two. It was probably the local tribesmen's final line of defence against invasion along the Trent Valley.

It is a prodigious feat of earth moving when you consider the workers were probably only possessed of antler picks, shoulder-blade shovels and baskets to move the earth; I don't suppose they stopped to admire the wonderful views.

HEDNESFORD
A RACE-TRACK IN A RESERVOIR

Access: Two miles from Castle Ring, signposted from Cannock.

Map Reference: Ordnance Survey map 120 (1:50,000); SK 016 123.

Of course it no longer has water in it! The Hednesford Raceway is well known as a centre for stock-car racing, but how many of its adherents realised that they were sitting in a reservoir?

It was constructed around 1880 by the South Staffs. Waterworks Company and was designed to store water pumped by engines on Cannock Chase down to Hednesford.

This is a mining area, and by 1952 subsidence had caused so many cracks and subsequent leakage that it was decided to dispense with it in its original guise, and it was put to the novel use it enjoys today.

GREAT HAYWOOD
THE ESSEX BRIDGE

> *Access:* Follow the A51 from Stone through Weston and turn right for Great Haywood. Take the side street on the right before the centre of the village.
>
> *Map Reference:* Ordnance Survey map 119 (1:50,000); SJ 995 226.

Washgate Bridge in the Moorlands might be the prettiest packhorse bridge in the county, but the Essex Bridge at Great Haywood is the longest packhorse bridge in England —even though it now has only 14 arches left of its original 40.

It was built in the seventeenth century by the Earl of Essex, hence its name. It was so long that there are recesses in the low walls over the buttresses to enable pedestrians to stand back out of the way of the wide panniers of the pack horse trains, or indeed out of the way of the entourages of the nobility, who might be off for a day's hunting or hawking on Cannock Chase.

SHALLOWFORD
IZAAK WALTON'S COTTAGE

Access: Follow the B5026 from Stone to Eccleshall, turn left for Norton
Bridge, then follow the signs.
Map Reference: Ordnance Survey map 119 (1:50,000); SJ 876 291.

In the seventeenth century, Izaak Walton, the author of *The Compleat Angler* (published in
1653) bought Halfhead Farm estate, which included this cottage standing on the banks of
the Meece Brook, between Stafford and Eccleshall.

It is thought that the building originally formed two dwellings, as each gable end has an
inglenook and chimney stack, and each bay has two doors, one to the front and one to the
rear.

When Izaak Walton died, he left the cottage to the Stafford Corporation with instructions
that the rent should be used for charitable purposes. The cottage was opened as a museum
in 1924.

The cottage has suffered a number of fires over the years and so has been considerably
restored, but an eighteenth-century print shows it to have been thatched, and with
eyebrow dormers. The aim is to show a typical seventeenth-century cottage, and the
charming garden is also typical of that period.

FORTON, NEAR NEWPORT
A CURIOUS CROSSING

Access: From Eccleshall to Newport on the A519, turn left at Forton, near
Newport, for Meretown. The bridge is reached after approximately
300 yards.

Map Reference: Ordnance Survey map 119 (1:50,000); SJ 756 209.

This will appeal to engineers, particularly canal enthusiasts. The Shropshire Union Canal
had to cross the River Meese between Forton and Meretown, and to do this a novel feat of
engineering was decided upon.

The road was realigned and combined with an aqueduct for the canal in a single bridge. It is
certainly unique in Staffordshire and very rare in the rest of the country.

It is constructed of ashlar stone, and is a very handsome monument to the canal era.

MERETOWN
AQUALATE CASTLE

Access: From Eccleshall to Newport on the A519, turn left at Forton, near Newport, for Meretown. Turn left at the 'T' junction in Meretown. The castle is visible on the left before reaching the Stafford-Newport road (visible only from the minor road after the River Meece Bridge at Meretown).

Map Reference: Ordnance Survey map 119 (1:50,000); SJ 767 194.

This building peeps romantically through the trees of the grounds of Aqualate Hall. It isn't actually a castle, but a red brick house with a round tower with battlements, and stepped gables.

The present Aqualate Hall itself was built 1927-30 to replace the previous Hall which was destroyed by fire in 1910.

GAILEY
THE TELFORD AQUEDUCT

> *Access:* Situated on the A5 from Cannock to Telford, approximately three
> miles west of Gailey roundabout.
>
> *Map Reference:* Ordnance Survey map 119 (1:50,000); SJ 873 107.

This compact and attractive little device crosses the A5 near Gailey, and carries the
Birmingham and Liverpool Junction canal.

The trough is made of five iron sections bolted together, the centre one proudly
announcing 'THOMAS TELFORD 1832'. Quite right that he should be proud of it.

By this century there became a distinct need for some more headroom and so the butments
had to be deepened (or the road was lowered, as I find it easier to think of it) to enable
something taller than a hay cart to get under it.

MOSELEY
MOSELEY OLD HALL

> *Access:* Signposted from the A449 Stafford-Wolverhampton road, to the left, about four miles after Gailey roundabout.
>
> *Map Reference:* Ordnance Survey map 119 (1:50,000); SJ 932 045.

The brick skin around this house successfully disguises the fact that this is an early half-timbered building and boasts several priest's holes. Its most romantic association is with the escape of the young King Charles II, who came to the house on 7 September 1651.

Thomas Whitgreave lived at Moseley and sheltered Charles, who by this time had cut his long, flowing hair and dyed his skin with walnut juice to try to disguise himself as a peasant; a hard task, as he towered above most men of that time, being "above two yards high."* Charles' bed is still in the house, and the priest's hole in which he hid, as the Parliamentarians called at Moseley Old Hall in their search for him, is still there.

The King was so grateful to the Whitgreaves for the risks which they took on his behalf that he awarded them a pension on his Restoration.

*as quoted from the 'Wanted' poster at the time.

WOMBOURNE
THE BRATCH

Access: From Wolverhampton take the A449 towards Wombourne, turn right at the island junction with the A463, and the locks are approximately one mile ahead.

Map Reference: Ordnance Survey map 130 (1:50,000); SJ 867 938.

Three-quarters-of-a-mile north-west of Womborne on the Staffordshire-Worcestershire canal is a unique flight of three locks constructed by Brindley and Dadford. They were originally designed as a staircase, but were then altered to three locks with ponds between.

The lock-keeper's office is a pretty octagonal building and the whole area a very pleasant place for a picnic lunch. There is a car park with a picnic area beside the canal.

WOMBOURNE
CHATEAU DE BRATCH

Access: Opposite the Bratch Locks.
Map Reference: Ordnance Survey map 130 (1:50,000); SJ 867 938.

This isn't what it seems at first sight! Set beside the car park and picnic area at Bratch is a red brick edifice with turrets at each corner, very reminiscent of a French chateau. It is actually Bilston Water Works, and was built in 1895 to supply water from boreholes to the town of Bilston.

BREWOOD
GIFFARD'S CROSS

Access: From the A5 Cannock-Telford road follow the signs to the left for Brewood, less than one mile west of Gailey roundabout. The cross is on the right, approximately one mile outside Brewood on the Codsall road.

Map Reference: Ordnance Survey map 119 (1:50,000); SJ 882 075.

This commemorates the death of a panther at the hands of Sir John Giffard; though where a panther sprang from in Chillington in the sixteenth century is a mystery in itself. Perhaps it was an escapee from a menagerie, or a forerunner of the genus Wild Beast of Exmoor.

Whilst out hunting with his crossbow, Sir John spied the beast and was able to shoot it, and thus save the life of a nearby mother and child. A cross was raised to commemorate such an unusual event.

The original cross has been removed, restored and resited in the grounds of Chillington Hall. The cross on the original site is a twentieth-century copy.

Sir John was an ancestor of those Giffards who helped Charles II escape after the battle of Worcester.

BREWOOD
SPEEDWELL HOUSE

> *Access:* Adjacent to the main cross-roads in the centre of Brewood.
> *Map Reference:* Ordnance Survey map 119 (1:50,000); SJ 883 088.

Speedwell certainly lived up to his name. He was a racehorse, and he lives for posterity because a local apothecary backed him at such excellent odds that he won enough money to enable him to build this rather excellent eighteenth-century Gothic residence in Brewood Main Street.

It makes me wonder if the apothecary popped one of his concoctions into Speedwell's oats!

BREWOOD
BEAT THAT!

Access: Both houses are in Dean Street, opposite the church.

Map Reference: Ordnance Survey map 119 (1:50,000); SJ 883 086.

In Brewood there are two houses, called 'The Chantry' and 'Westgate'. Incorporated into the wall of Westgate (nearest the camera) is the mask of a figure with its tongue sticking out, pointing towards The Chantry, the third, more humble, building.

According to legend these two houses were owned by two sisters in whom the tide of sibling rivalry flowed very strong, and the owner of Westgate had the mask put there to show the owner of The Chantry exactly what she thought of her.

BREWOOD
OLD SMITHY COTTAGE

> *Access:* A little further down from 'The Chantry' and 'Westgate' at the end of Dean Street.
>
> *Map Reference:* Ordnance Survey map 119 (1:50,000); SJ 883 086.

Old Smithy House in Brewood is a rather grand town house, and adjoining it is a row of early timber-framed cottages; the whole presenting a very pleasing picture. The last of the row, Old Smithy Cottage, is the most interesting because it claims to date from 1350. The plaque, which until recently announced this to the world, has been removed because it was deemed to be unsafe. The owners are hoping to replace it in the near future.

INDEX